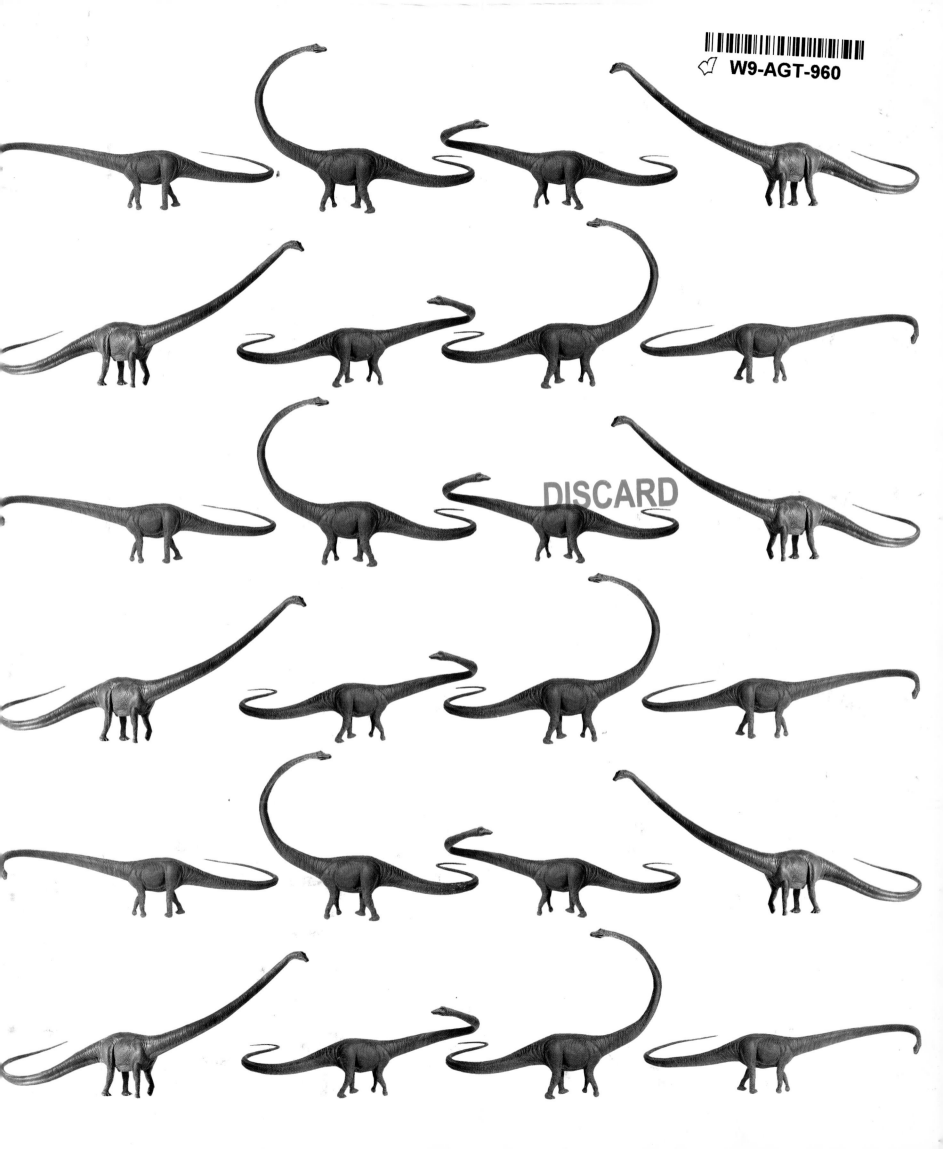

A DORLING KINDERSLEY BOOK

Project editor Monica Byles
U.S. editor and researcher Mary Ann Lynch
Art editor Penny Britchfield
Designer Peter Radcliffe
Managing editor Jane Yorke
Managing art editor Chris Scollen
Production Louise Barratt and Neil Palfreyman

Illustration Simone Boni/L.R. Galante
Barosaurus **model** Jeremy Hunt/Centaur Studios
Model photography Dave King
Museum photography Lynton Gardiner

First American Edition, 1992
10 9 8 7 6 5 4 3 2 1

Published in the United States by
Dorling Kindersley, Inc., 232 Madison Avenue
New York, New York 10016

Reproduced by Colourscan, Singapore
Printed and bound in Italy by Graphicom

Library of Congress Cataloging-in-Publication Data

Lindsay, William
    Barosaurus / William Lindsay. —1st American ed.
        p.   cm.
    Includes index.
    Summary: Describes the discovery and mounting of fossil evidence
for the dinosaur called Barosaurus and examines what this evidence suggests
about its appearance and behavior.
        ISBN 1-56458-123-3
        1. Barosaurus — Juvenile literature.   [1. Barosaurus.
2. Dinosaurs. 3. Fossils. 4. Paleontology.] I. Title.
QE862.S3L55 1992
567.9'7—dc20   92-52819
                                                                      CIP
                                                                      AC

AMERICAN MUSEUM OF NATURAL HISTORY

Barosaurus

William Lindsay

Consultant Mark Norell

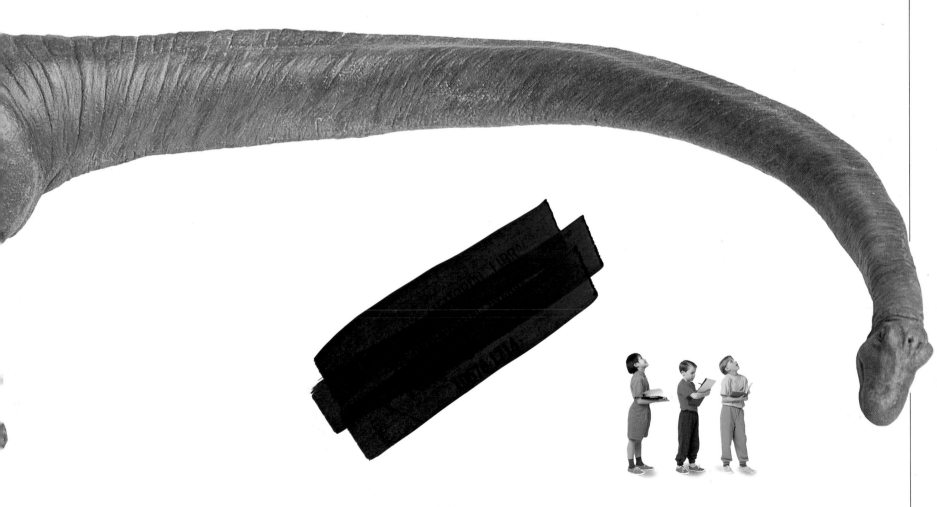

DORLING KINDERSLEY, INC.
London • New York • Stuttgart

CONTENTS

INTRODUCTION

Dinosaurs such as the colossal *Barosaurus* – one of the largest ever to have lived – dominated the continents of the world for over 150 million years. Even today, their descendants, the birds, rule the sky. Dinosaurs may look like science-fiction creatures, but we know they were not imaginary because we find their hard bones and teeth preserved in rock as stony fossils.
Fossils are our only real evidence of extinct dinosaurs. Their rocky skeletons show how large they grew, and fossil footprints tell us something about how they moved. By studying the shape of their bones, we can even tell which dinosaurs were close evolutionary relatives. But fossils don't tell us all we would like to know about how these prehistoric creatures behaved.
As Director of the Fossil Hall Renovation at the American Museum of Natural History, I work with others to decide how to mount dinosaur specimens. The *Barosaurus* you will read about in this book is part of our newest exhibit. It has been mounted rearing up on its hind legs to protect its baby from an attacking *Allosaurus*. Would *Barosaurus* have been able to rear up like this? Perhaps. Its legs and the front part of its tail were strongly constructed with powerful bones and muscles. But no one knows for sure. It is the job of fossil experts – paleontologists – to make educated guesses about what dinosaurs might have been able to do, and how they might have moved and acted.

Lowell Dingus
Director, Fossil Hall Renovation,
American Museum of Natural History

PREHISTORIC WORLD

Dinosaurs are one of the most amazing groups of animals that ever lived. Although these great animals became extinct 65 million years ago (except for their descendants, the birds), scientists today find many clues to the past lives of the dinosaurs in their fossil remains left behind. Dinosaurs were reptiles – they laid eggs, had scaly skin, and lived on land. Dinosaurs ruled the Earth for over 150 million years. One of the most gigantic dinosaurs was *Barosaurus*, a plant-eater. It lived about 150 million years ago, during the Jurassic Period of the Earth's history.

Barosaurus (barrow-saw-rus) means "heavy lizard."

Prehistoric giants
Dinosaurs are the biggest animals ever to have lived on land. However, some dinosaurs were only as small as a chicken. *Barosaurus* was a sauropod, a plant-eater with a huge barrel-shaped body.

Grouped by bones
Dinosaurs are divided into two groups by the shape and position of their hip bones. "Bird-hipped" or ornithischian dinosaurs had the two lower pelvic bones pointing backward and down.
   "Lizard-hipped" or saurischian dinosaurs, like *Barosaurus*, had one of the two lower bones pointing forward and the other pointing backward. All of the bird-hipped dinosaurs were plant-eaters. The lizard-hipped dinosaurs were both plant-eaters and meat-eaters.

Barosaurus had a neck 30 ft (9 m) long, even longer than the necks of *Diplodocus* and *Apatosaurus*, its close relatives. With such a long neck, plant-eating *Barosaurus* could reach into the treetops.

Heterodontosaurus "bird-hipped" dinosaur

Struthiomimus "lizard-hipped" dinosaur

Unlike some other primitive reptiles, which have sprawling legs, dinosaurs stood on straight legs.

Dinosaurs through the ages

Different dinosaurs appeared and died out over three periods of the Earth's history. *Barosaurus* lived in the Jurassic Period.

TRIASSIC PERIOD	JURASSIC PERIOD	CRETACEOUS PERIOD
245–208 million years ago	208–145 million years ago	145–65 million years ago

Prehistoric feeder

Barosaurus was a plant-eater, or herbivore. It had a huge barrel-shaped body, designed to hold the large amounts of food it ate every day. *Barosaurus* had special peg-shaped teeth to snip off plant food. Meat-eating dinosaurs, or carnivores, such as *Allosaurus*, had sharp teeth and claws for slashing and tearing meat.

Dinosaur skin

Scientists have found fossilized impressions of dinosaur skin. It was tough and covered in knobby scales, like the skin of modern crocodiles.

Scaly reptile skin

Barosaurus had a whiplike tail, which it may have used to frighten off attackers.

Barosaurus weighed more than eight elephants. It had sturdy, pillarlike legs, which ended in elephantlike feet with five toes. Its rear legs were even bigger than its front legs.

FOSSIL TREASURES

One of the world's richest hoards of dinosaur fossil treasure was discovered among stony, barren hills in Utah. A wide river flowed there in the Jurassic Period, where dinosaurs gathered to eat and drink. Over many years, dinosaur remains were buried under mud and sand and were slowly transformed into fossils.

In 1908, Earl Douglass, a fossil collector, first came to investigate the site for the Carnegie Museum of Natural History. Four years later, he found an almost complete skeleton of *Barosaurus*. Douglass' discoveries were so important that in 1915 the dinosaur graveyard was made a national monument.

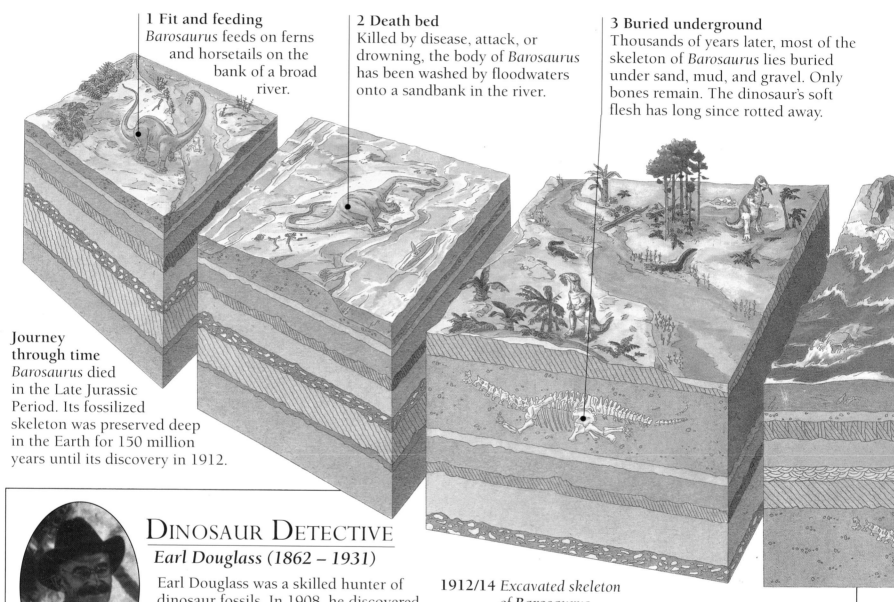

1 Fit and feeding
Barosaurus feeds on ferns and horsetails on the bank of a broad river.

2 Death bed
Killed by disease, attack, or drowning, the body of *Barosaurus* has been washed by floodwaters onto a sandbank in the river.

3 Buried underground
Thousands of years later, most of the skeleton of *Barosaurus* lies buried under sand, mud, and gravel. Only bones remain. The dinosaur's soft flesh has long since rotted away.

Journey through time
Barosaurus died in the Late Jurassic Period. Its fossilized skeleton was preserved deep in the Earth for 150 million years until its discovery in 1912.

DINOSAUR DETECTIVE
Earl Douglass (1862 – 1931)

Earl Douglass was a skilled hunter of dinosaur fossils. In 1908, he discovered the important fossil site later named Dinosaur National Monument. For 16 years he worked to establish the Monument as a unique working museum.

1862	*Born in Medford, Minnesota.*
1902	*Joined the staff of the Carnegie Museum, Pittsburgh, Pennsylvania.*
1909	*Found and began to excavate Apatosaurus.*
1909/24	*Excavated Apatosaurus, Stegosaurus, Allosaurus, Diplodocus, Camarasaurus, Barosaurus, and Camptosaurus.*
1912/14	*Excavated skeleton of Barosaurus.*
1914	*Completed mount of Apatosaurus at the Carnegie Museum.*
1924	*Left the Dinosaur National Monument.*
1931	*Died in Salt Lake City, Utah, age 69.*

Fossil hunter
Earl Douglass, standing next to a partly excavated Diplodocus skeleton in 1922.

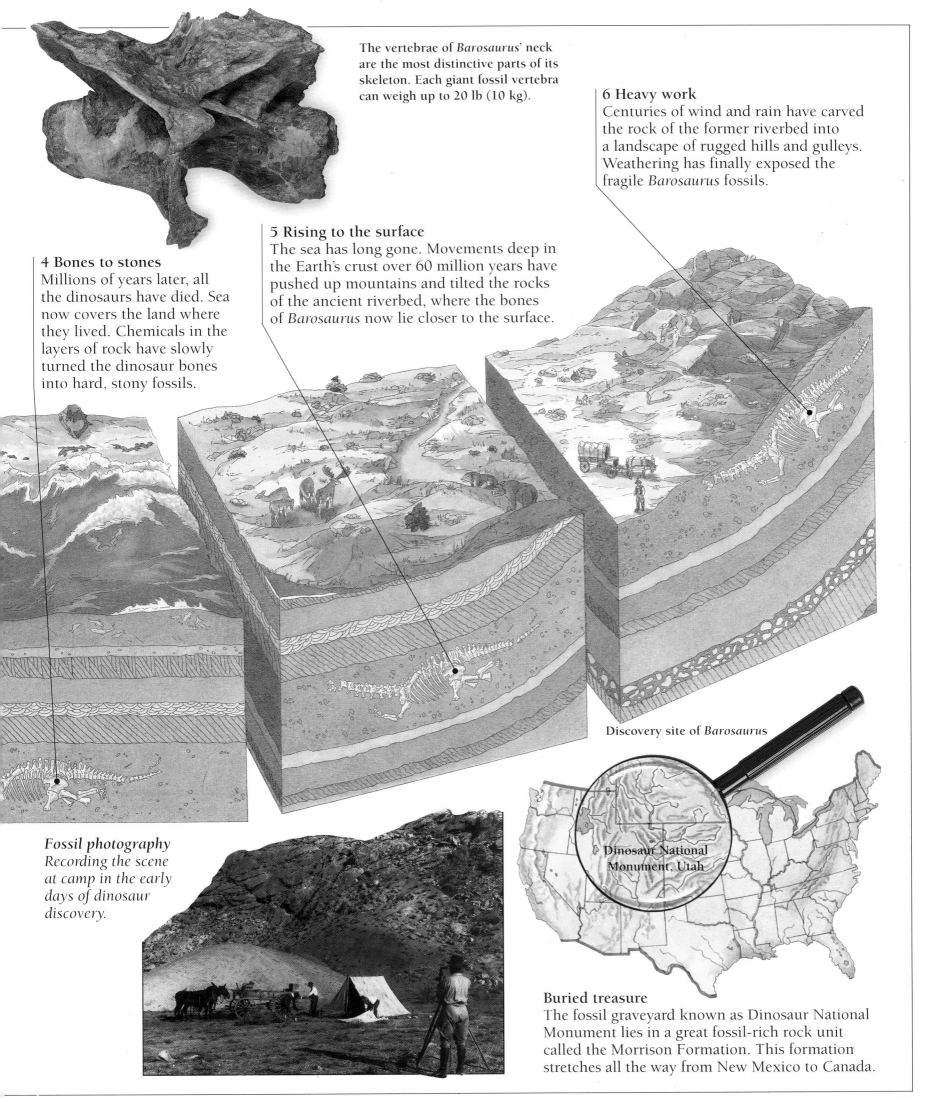

The vertebrae of *Barosaurus'* neck are the most distinctive parts of its skeleton. Each giant fossil vertebra can weigh up to 20 lb (10 kg).

6 Heavy work
Centuries of wind and rain have carved the rock of the former riverbed into a landscape of rugged hills and gulleys. Weathering has finally exposed the fragile *Barosaurus* fossils.

5 Rising to the surface
The sea has long gone. Movements deep in the Earth's crust over 60 million years have pushed up mountains and tilted the rocks of the ancient riverbed, where the bones of *Barosaurus* now lie closer to the surface.

4 Bones to stones
Millions of years later, all the dinosaurs have died. Sea now covers the land where they lived. Chemicals in the layers of rock have slowly turned the dinosaur bones into hard, stony fossils.

Fossil photography
Recording the scene at camp in the early days of dinosaur discovery.

Discovery site of *Barosaurus*

Dinosaur National Monument, Utah

Buried treasure
The fossil graveyard known as Dinosaur National Monument lies in a great fossil-rich rock unit called the Morrison Formation. This formation stretches all the way from New Mexico to Canada.

11

DINOSAUR JIGSAW

Earl Douglass and his team of dinosaur diggers took two long years to excavate the bones of *Barosaurus* on behalf of the Carnegie Museum in Pittsburgh, Pennsylvania. The Museum, however, traded sections of the skeleton with two other museums needing parts to help complete their own sauropod specimens. The fossil bones might still be separated today, were it not for the determination of the dinosaur hunter Barnum Brown. He succeeded in reuniting the complete *Barosaurus* skeleton at the American Museum of Natural History in New York.

Cracks in the ancient fossil bones were repaired with glue and plaster.

Digging for dinosaurs
Douglass and his men used shovels, hammers, picks, chisels, and even dynamite to dig the fossil skeleton of *Barosaurus* from its rocky grave.

Controlled explosion
Dynamite was needed to blast away some of the hardest rock. This was formed from the mud and sand of the ancient riverbed, now turned to solid stone.

Grid system
The fossil bones were excavated from a steep quarry face. A grid was painted on the rock to make it easier to record where each bone was found.

Neck vertebra, slightly crushed during fossilization.

Rounded end of bone fit snugly into the hollow of the next vertebra.

Plaster jackets
Once exposed, the fragile bones were wrapped in a protective jacket of plaster and burlap. When the plaster was dry, the heavy bones were hauled up the steep rockface.

Slow sled
Mules dragged the bones in their plaster jackets out of the quarry by sled. Many trips were needed to remove all the fossil bones.

Back vertebra, about 24 in (60 cm) long

Rock waste
Tons of rock were chipped away from the rockface during the excavation. Waste rubble was pushed in carts along a short railway and then dumped down the steep hillside.

Fossil trading

Barnum Brown of the American Museum of Natural History in New York had reunited all the parts of the *Barosaurus* skeleton by 1929.

American Museum of Natural History, New York

This museum used money and fossils to "buy" all parts of the *Barosaurus* skeleton.

Carnegie Museum, Pittsburgh, Pennsylvania

This museum had received part of *Barosaurus'* tail from the University of Utah.

Smithsonian Institution, Washington, D.C.

The Smithsonian owned bones from the neck and body of *Barosaurus* and part of a limb.

University of Utah, Salt Lake City, Utah

The university museum received $5,000 and a fossil horse skeleton in exchange for their *Barosaurus* parts.

Dinosaur National Monument, Utah

The original site of excavation of *Barosaurus*. Its fossils were later split up among three different museums.

Basement storage

The *Barosaurus* bones were stored in the basement of the AMNH, where they were available for study. Sixty years later, the Museum finally decided to prepare the fossils for display.

Bones were stored on open shelves in the Museum's basement.

All pieces of fossil from the skeleton were kept together.

These shelves were filled with *Barosaurus* vertebrae.

DINOSAUR DETECTIVE

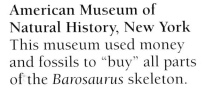

Barnum Brown (1873 – 1963)

Barnum Brown was a great dinosaur hunter and collector. In his years at the American Museum of Natural History in New York, he filled the dinosaur halls with many of the fossil skeletons he had excavated. Although he did not discover *Barosaurus* himself, he knew that this was an important specimen to acquire for the Museum's dinosaur collection.

1873   *Born in Carbondale, Kansas.*
1897   *Joined the staff of the American Museum of Natural History (AMNH) in New York.*
1902   *Discovered the world's first known specimen of **Tyrannosaurus rex**.*
1908   *Discovered a second, more complete, specimen of **Tyrannosaurus rex**.*
1910   *Began collecting dinosaur remains along the Red Deer River, Alberta, Canada.*
1912   *Discovered the skeletons of the duck-billed dinosaur, **Corythosaurus**, and the horned dinosaur, **Monoclonius**.*
1916   *Completed dinosaur hunting along the Red Deer River.*
1929   *Gathered the separated parts of the **Barosaurus** skeleton at the AMNH.*
1934   *Excavated the remains of over 20 sauropod dinosaurs at Howe Quarry, Wyoming.*
1942   *Retired from the AMNH.*
1963   *Died, age 89, in New York.*

DINOSAUR DOUBLE

The skeleton of *Barosaurus* was finally taken out of storage 80 years after its discovery. Museum scientists planned to put the bones on display. They wanted to mount the skeleton rearing up on its back legs, defending its young against an attacking *Allosaurus*. Because the fossil bones were fragile and too heavy to display in this way, the scientists decided to make a lightweight plastic replica of the skeleton. Once the fossils had been restored and any missing bones modeled from special clay, casting could begin.

Materials used to cast the fossilized bones

Liquid rubber

Liquid plastic

Brushes

Cleaning fluid for brushes

1 Building dams
First, "dams" made of cardboard are used to divide the surface of each fossil bone, or group of bones. The dams stand like walls on the surface of the bone, and split it into sections. More dams are needed if the bone shape is complicated. The dams give flat edges to the molds, so that all the parts of a replica bone will fit together neatly.

2 Making a rubber mold
Each part of the fossil bone and dam is now painted with layers of liquid rubber. When the rubber sets, it forms a perfect, flexible mold of the original bone's surface. The rubber mold is then peeled away from the fossil.

3 Supporting the mold
The rubber mold is strengthened with cotton gauze. A plastic jacket is made to support the outside.

4 Casting the bones
Next, the inside of the rubber mold is coated with liquid plastic. The plastic will duplicate every detail that has been molded from the fossil's surface.

5 Assembling the cast
Sheets of fiberglass are added to the plastic to make light but strong casts of the fossil. The cast sections are then joined together to recreate the entire bone's shape.

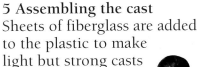

6 Filling the cast
The hollow bone cast is made even stronger by pouring in a special liquid foam plastic. This foam hardens to form a tough honeycomb center.

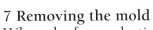

7 Removing the mold
When the foam plastic has hardened inside the cast, the rubber mold and its supporting jacket are peeled away from the outside. At last, a perfectly shaped plastic copy of the original fossil bone is revealed.

8 Finishing touches
Finally, the rough edges left by the joints between the separate mold sections are carefully filed away. The plastic bone is then painted to match the colors of the original fossil.

9 Measuring up
The replica fossils are measured against a chart of the whole skeleton. Each plastic bone is then matched up against its neighbors to check the fit. Only when all the bones are complete – more than 200 – will the lightweight *Barosaurus* skeleton be ready for assembly in the museum.

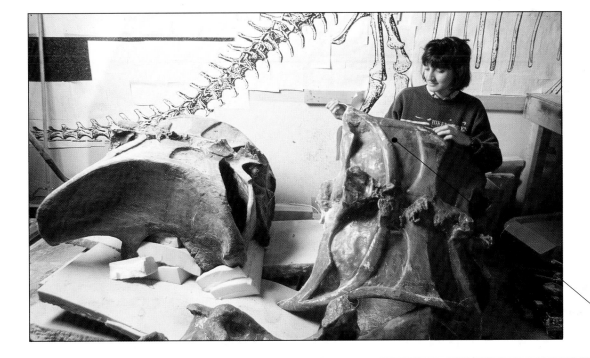

BUILDING BAROSAURUS

The *Barosaurus* skeleton was hauled by truck from Canada to New York for assembly in its new home at the American Museum of Natural History. Here, the task of assembling the *Barosaurus* mount in its unique rearing pose required expert construction skills. Specialists from many different fields – artists and model-makers, paleontologists, and engineers – all came together to reconstruct a dramatic scene that may have taken place around 150 million years ago.

A few of the many dinosaur builders whose varied skills helped to assemble the rearing *Barosaurus* mount.

1 The skeleton arrives
Huge trucks deliver the replica *Barosaurus* bones safely to the museum.

2 Checking the plans
Inside the museum, detailed plans are consulted at each stage of the dinosaur's assembly. Even a small mistake in the positioning of body sections would be difficult to correct, once building is complete.

3 Dinosaur rib cage
The giant rib cage is unloaded in one piece. The ribs show the barrel shape of *Barosaurus'* vast body.

4 Neck section
The massive neck section is gently removed from the trailer. The giant vertebrae are already threaded onto a supporting steel pipe.

5 Rocky base
A natural landscape is pieced together to make a realistic base for the *Barosaurus* mount. Latex rubber was painted onto rocky ground in Montana. When set, the rubber was peeled away and used as a mold to make a fiberglass cast, or "land-peel."

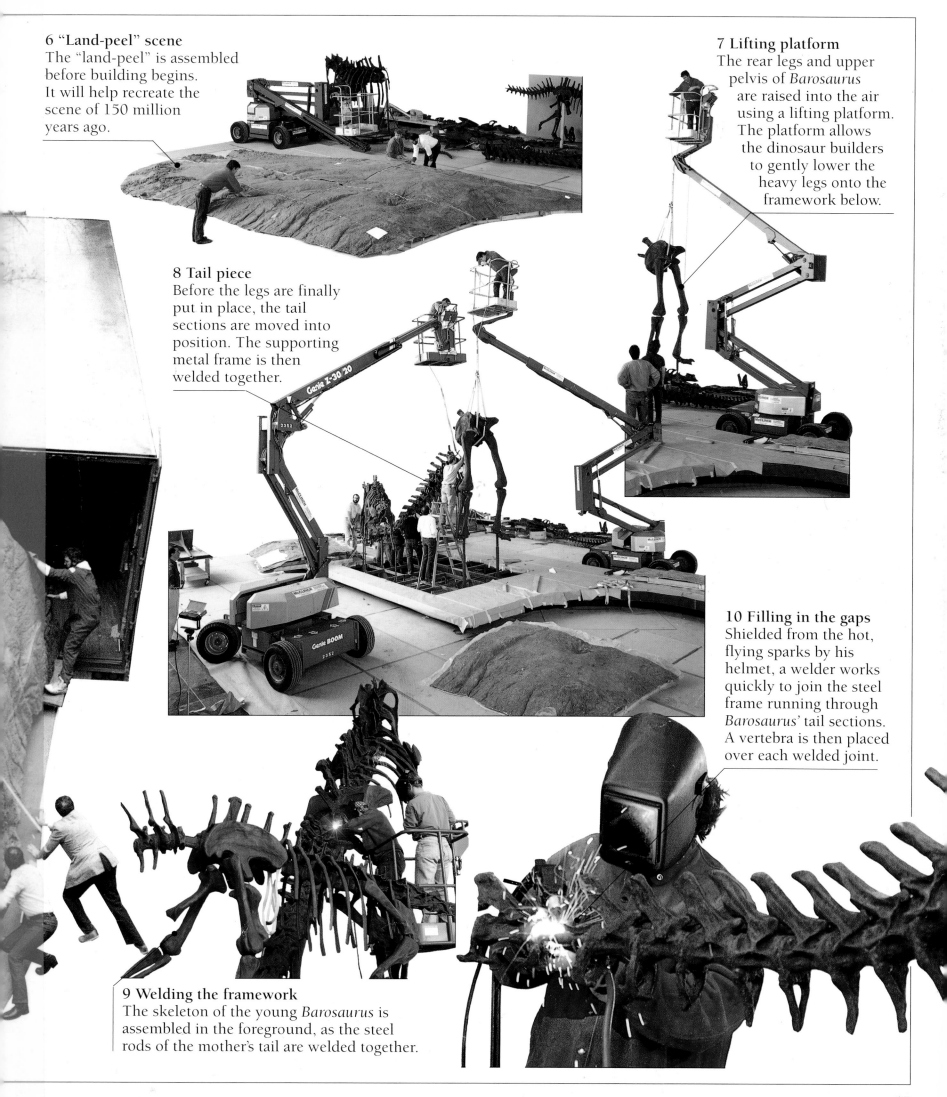

6 "Land-peel" scene
The "land-peel" is assembled before building begins. It will help recreate the scene of 150 million years ago.

7 Lifting platform
The rear legs and upper pelvis of *Barosaurus* are raised into the air using a lifting platform. The platform allows the dinosaur builders to gently lower the heavy legs onto the framework below.

8 Tail piece
Before the legs are finally put in place, the tail sections are moved into position. The supporting metal frame is then welded together.

10 Filling in the gaps
Shielded from the hot, flying sparks by his helmet, a welder works quickly to join the steel frame running through *Barosaurus'* tail sections. A vertebra is then placed over each welded joint.

9 Welding the framework
The skeleton of the young *Barosaurus* is assembled in the foreground, as the steel rods of the mother's tail are welded together.

17

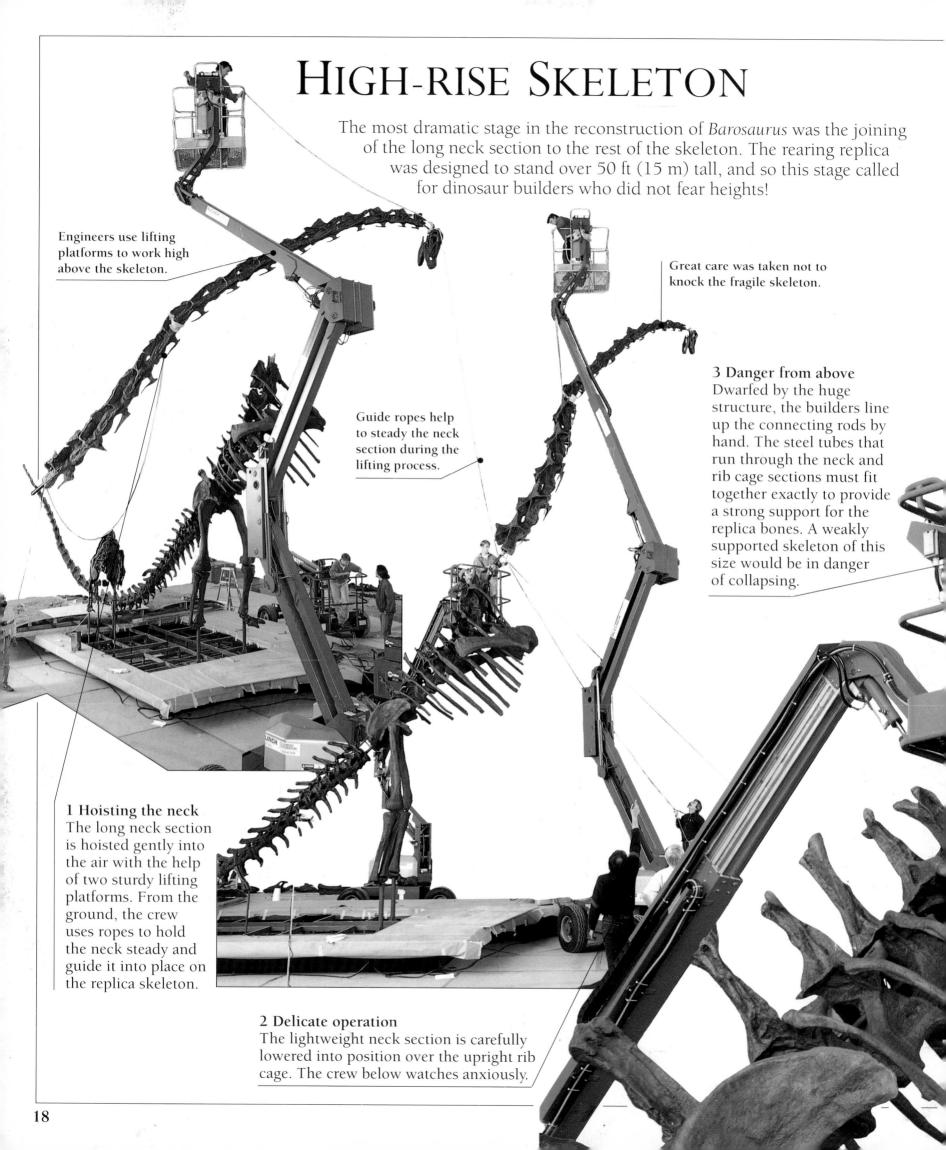

HIGH-RISE SKELETON

The most dramatic stage in the reconstruction of *Barosaurus* was the joining of the long neck section to the rest of the skeleton. The rearing replica was designed to stand over 50 ft (15 m) tall, and so this stage called for dinosaur builders who did not fear heights!

Engineers use lifting platforms to work high above the skeleton.

Great care was taken not to knock the fragile skeleton.

Guide ropes help to steady the neck section during the lifting process.

3 Danger from above
Dwarfed by the huge structure, the builders line up the connecting rods by hand. The steel tubes that run through the neck and rib cage sections must fit together exactly to provide a strong support for the replica bones. A weakly supported skeleton of this size would be in danger of collapsing.

1 Hoisting the neck
The long neck section is hoisted gently into the air with the help of two sturdy lifting platforms. From the ground, the crew uses ropes to hold the neck steady and guide it into place on the replica skeleton.

2 Delicate operation
The lightweight neck section is carefully lowered into position over the upright rib cage. The crew below watches anxiously.

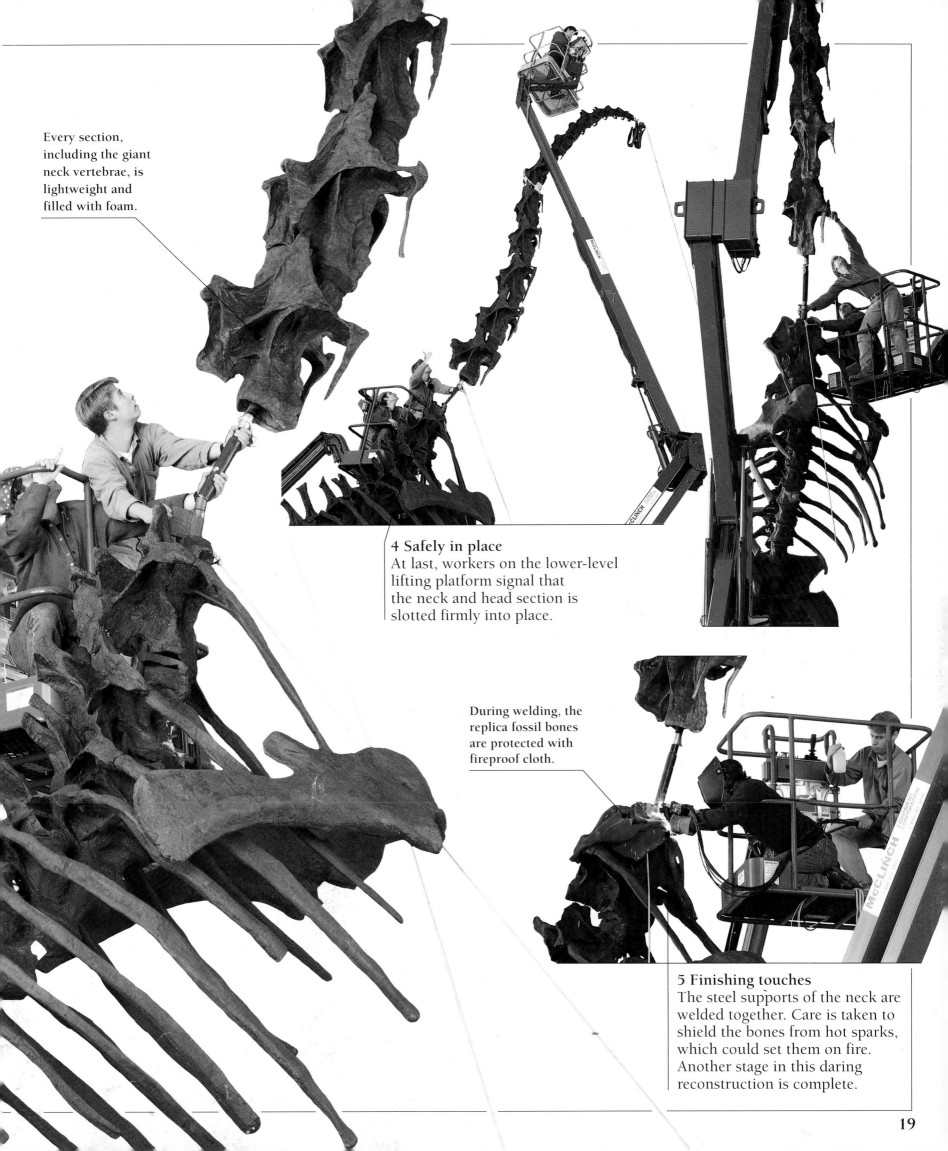

Every section, including the giant neck vertebrae, is lightweight and filled with foam.

4 Safely in place
At last, workers on the lower-level lifting platform signal that the neck and head section is slotted firmly into place.

During welding, the replica fossil bones are protected with fireproof cloth.

5 Finishing touches
The steel supports of the neck are welded together. Care is taken to shield the bones from hot sparks, which could set them on fire. Another stage in this daring reconstruction is complete.

ATTACK AND DEFENSE

F ew animals would have had anything to fear from the plant-eating *Barosaurus*. Large and lumbering, the dinosaur would have browsed through foliage paying little attention to its neighbors. But the giant *Barosaurus* would have feared the fierce meat-eaters, such as *Allosaurus*, which prowled around the sites where plant-eating dinosaurs grazed, waiting for the chance to attack a sickly or unprotected youngster.

The sensational display of fossil skeletons at the American Museum of Natural History demonstrates one idea of how *Barosaurus* may have defended her young against attack by a hungry predator, 150 million years ago.

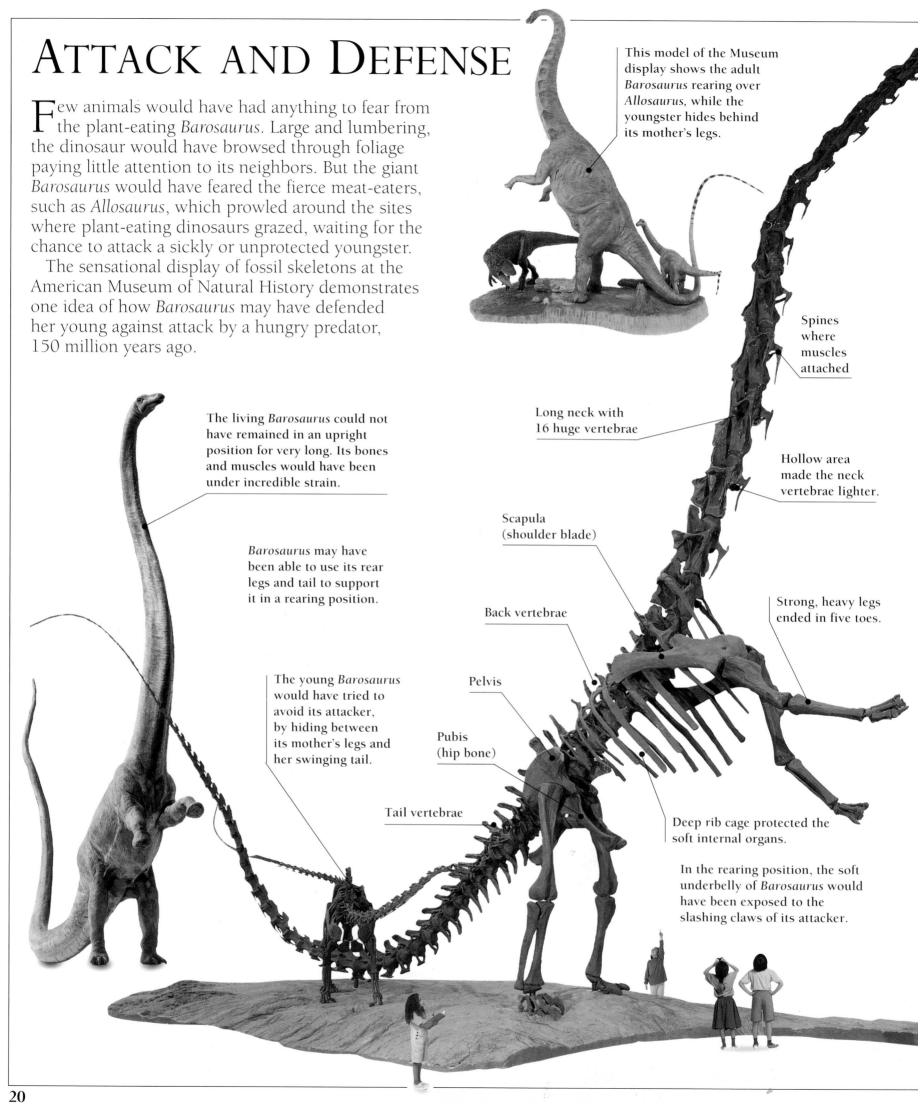

This model of the Museum display shows the adult *Barosaurus* rearing over *Allosaurus*, while the youngster hides behind its mother's legs.

Spines where muscles attached

Long neck with 16 huge vertebrae

Hollow area made the neck vertebrae lighter.

The living *Barosaurus* could not have remained in an upright position for very long. Its bones and muscles would have been under incredible strain.

Barosaurus may have been able to use its rear legs and tail to support it in a rearing position.

Scapula (shoulder blade)

Strong, heavy legs ended in five toes.

Back vertebrae

The young *Barosaurus* would have tried to avoid its attacker, by hiding between its mother's legs and her swinging tail.

Pelvis

Pubis (hip bone)

Tail vertebrae

Deep rib cage protected the soft internal organs.

In the rearing position, the soft underbelly of *Barosaurus* would have been exposed to the slashing claws of its attacker.

The head of *Barosaurus* was modeled on that of *Diplodocus*, its close relative. No fossil skull bones of *Barosaurus* have been found.

Fast runner
The replica skeleton of *Allosaurus* is mounted in a running position, with its tail outstretched for balance.

1 Base framework
The body and tail are attached to the legs and pelvis, which are mounted on a metal framework.

Allosaurus had small, powerful front limbs. Each hand had three sharp claws.

2 Arms in place
The bones of the shoulders, arms, and the dangerous claws are welded into place.

Allosaurus stood upright like a bird, on three long toes.

Hungry hunter
150 million years ago, *Allosaurus* was the chief predator in the land that is now North America. *Allosaurus* was 36 ft (11 m) long and weighed 1.5 tons (1.5 tonnes). It posed a deadly threat to a young *Barosaurus*.

Tail held high for balance

Large, powerful legs for running after prey

3 Skull and bones
The skull of *Allosaurus*, four times longer than a human head, is placed at the end of the smoothly curved neck. The replica skeleton is now complete.

Jaws lined with razor-sharp teeth for cutting and tearing flesh

The natural landscape base helps to set the scene of the Jurassic Period.

ON THE MOVE

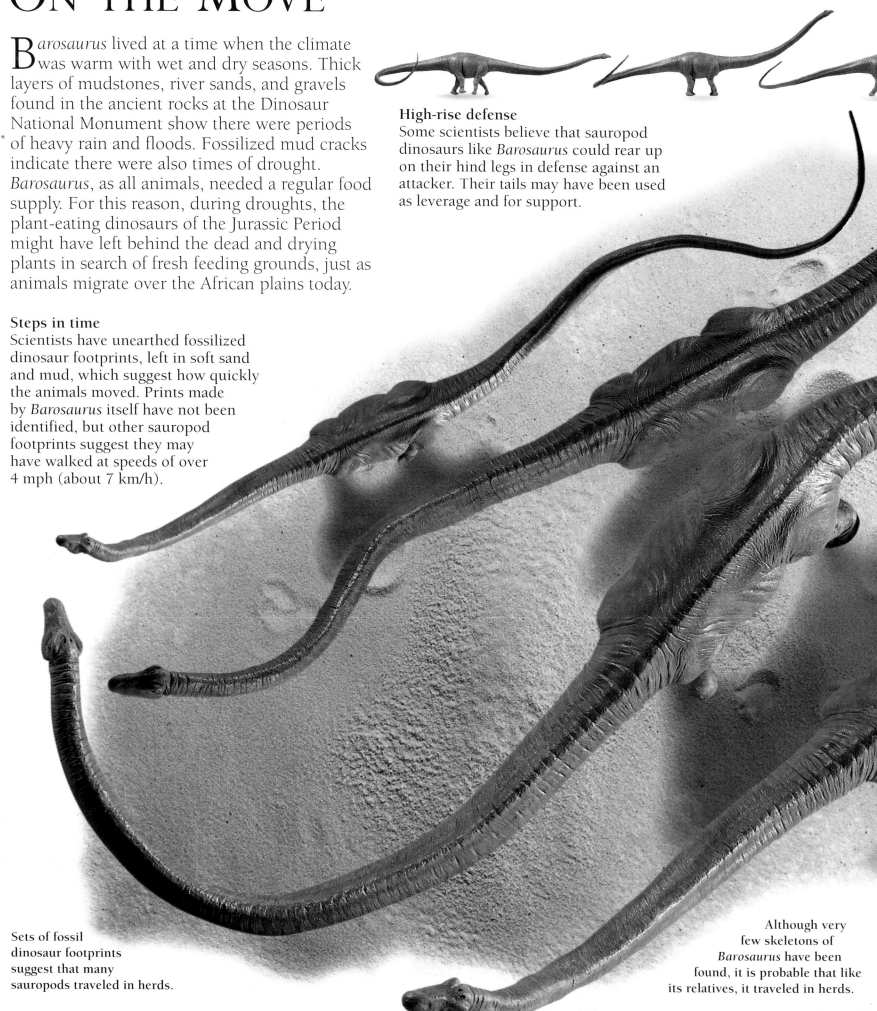

Barosaurus lived at a time when the climate was warm with wet and dry seasons. Thick layers of mudstones, river sands, and gravels found in the ancient rocks at the Dinosaur National Monument show there were periods of heavy rain and floods. Fossilized mud cracks indicate there were also times of drought. Barosaurus, as all animals, needed a regular food supply. For this reason, during droughts, the plant-eating dinosaurs of the Jurassic Period might have left behind the dead and drying plants in search of fresh feeding grounds, just as animals migrate over the African plains today.

Steps in time
Scientists have unearthed fossilized dinosaur footprints, left in soft sand and mud, which suggest how quickly the animals moved. Prints made by Barosaurus itself have not been identified, but other sauropod footprints suggest they may have walked at speeds of over 4 mph (about 7 km/h).

High-rise defense
Some scientists believe that sauropod dinosaurs like Barosaurus could rear up on their hind legs in defense against an attacker. Their tails may have been used as leverage and for support.

Sets of fossil dinosaur footprints suggest that many sauropods traveled in herds.

Although very few skeletons of Barosaurus have been found, it is probable that like its relatives, it traveled in herds.

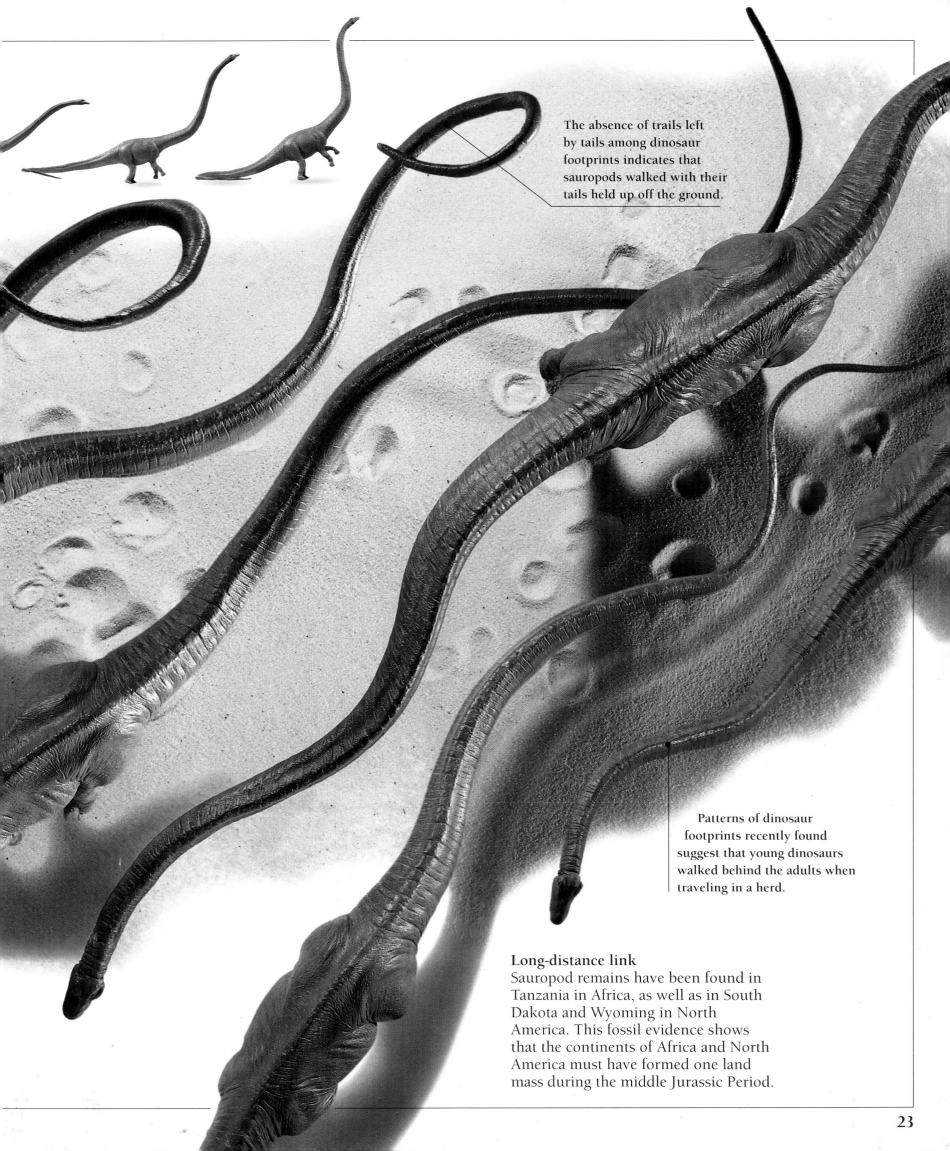

The absence of trails left
by tails among dinosaur
footprints indicates that
sauropods walked with their
tails held up off the ground.

Patterns of dinosaur
footprints recently found
suggest that young dinosaurs
walked behind the adults when
traveling in a herd.

Long-distance link
Sauropod remains have been found in
Tanzania in Africa, as well as in South
Dakota and Wyoming in North
America. This fossil evidence shows
that the continents of Africa and North
America must have formed one land
mass during the middle Jurassic Period.

GREEDY GIANT

Barosaurus was a giant plant-eater living during the Jurassic Period. The warm, wet climate produced the great quantity of plants needed to satisfy this dinosaur's monster appetite. Although there were no grasses, *Barosaurus* and other herbivores fed on ferns, horsetails, ginkgos, conifers, and many other plants that still grow today.

Diplodocus

Gentle grazers
Many dinosaurs grazed with *Barosaurus* on the lush floodplain or along the winding river.

Barosaurus needed to eat huge amounts of plant food every day to fuel its gigantic body.

Stony stomach
Barosaurus raked in plant matter with its peglike teeth and then swallowed it whole. Once in its stomach, the food was ground into a thick paste by hard, shiny pebbles called gastroliths.

Barosaurus swallowed stones to grind up its food, just as some birds do today.

Treetop browser
The long neck of *Barosaurus* was useful for feeding on leaves high in the treetops. Instead of browsing at such a dizzying height, it might have preferred leaves from lower branches.

Whiplash tail
Barosaurus stayed on constant alert when near a prowling *Allosaurus*. If the *Allosaurus* threatened to attack its young, *Barosaurus* could whip its tail to keep the predator at bay.

Apatosaurus

Camptosaurus

Ferocious hunter
Allosaurus was a fierce carnivore that hunted plant-eaters.

Riverside feeders
Groups of *Apatosaurus* and a *Camptosaurus* browsed by the riverside.

Stegosaurus

Hungry herbivores
Both *Stegosaurus* with its bony plates, and large herds of the long-necked *Diplodocus*, grazed together on the plains.

Fast movers
Small *Dryosaurus* lived in groups. They relied on speed to escape from danger.

The long neck of *Barosaurus* allowed its head to move in all directions, as the animal watched for danger.

If a baby *Barosaurus* survived disease and attack, and found enough to eat, it might have lived to be 100 years old.

Baby food
The young *Barosaurus* stayed close to its parent, feeding on low-growing leaves and ground plants, such as ferns.

BAROSAURUS FACT FILE

- **Specimen number:** AMNH 6341
- **Excavated by:** Earl Douglass
- **Excavation:** 1912–1914, at Dinosaur National Monument, Utah
- **Bones found:** Four-fifths of skeleton
- **Where displayed:** American Museum of Natural History (AMNH), New York
- **When constructed:** 1991; lightweight replica bones used in place of original heavy fossils

- **Lived:** 150 million years ago, Jurassic Period
- **Family:** Diplodocids, part of sauropod group
- **Dinosaur type:** Lizard-hipped (saurischian)
- **Maximum life span:** Perhaps 100 years
- **Diet:** Rough plant material
- **Weight when alive:** Over 59 tons (about 60 tonnes)
- **Height:** Over 50 ft (15 m)
- **Length:** 80 ft (24 m)
- **Top speed:** Over 4 mph (about 7 km/h)

🏛 ON THE MUSEUM TRAIL 🏛

A museum guide to sauropod specimens
A partial listing of collections, including both fossils and replica casts of fossils.

UNITED STATES
(*Diplodocus*) Pratt Museum (Amherst College), Amherst, Massachusetts
(*Apatosaurus*) Field Museum of Natural History, Chicago, Illinois
(*Diplodocus*) Houston Museum of Natural Sciences, Houston, Texas
(*Apatosaurus, Diplodocus*) Dinosaur National Monument, Jensen, Utah
(*Apatosaurus*) The Geological Museum, Laramie, Wyoming
(*Apatosaurus, Barosaurus*) American Museum of Natural History, New York, New York
(*Apatosaurus*) Peabody Museum of Natural History, Yale University, Connecticut
(*Supersaurus*) Academy of Natural Sciences, Philadelphia, Pennsylvania
(*Apatosaurus, Diplodocus*) Carnegie Museum of Natural History, Pittsburgh, Pennsylvania

Sauropod specimens may also be found in museums in Argentina, Canada, China, France, Germany, Italy, Japan, Mexico, Mongolia, Morocco, Russia, Spain, and the United Kingdom.

Unique display
The AMNH in New York has the only *Barosaurus* skeleton on display in the world. A replica made of plastic and metal, the dinosaur rears up in the air, protecting its young from an attacking *Allosaurus*.

(*Supersaurus*) Earth Science Museum, Brigham Young University, Provo, Utah
(*Diplodocus*) The Science Museum of Minnesota, St Paul, Minnesota
(*Barosaurus*) Utah Museum of Natural History, University of Utah, Salt Lake City, Utah
(*Diplodocus*) Utah Natural History State Museum, Vernal, Utah
(*Diplodocus*) National Museum of Natural History, Smithsonian Institution, Washington, D.C.

Barosaurus had a neck 18 ft (9 m) long. This animal lived around 150 million years ago, during the Jurassic Period.

Dinosaur world

Different kinds of dinosaurs lived in different parts of the world, while the landscape and climate slowly changed. The sauropod dinosaurs were the largest animals ever to live on land. This map shows some areas where the fossil remains of *Barosaurus* and its family have been found.

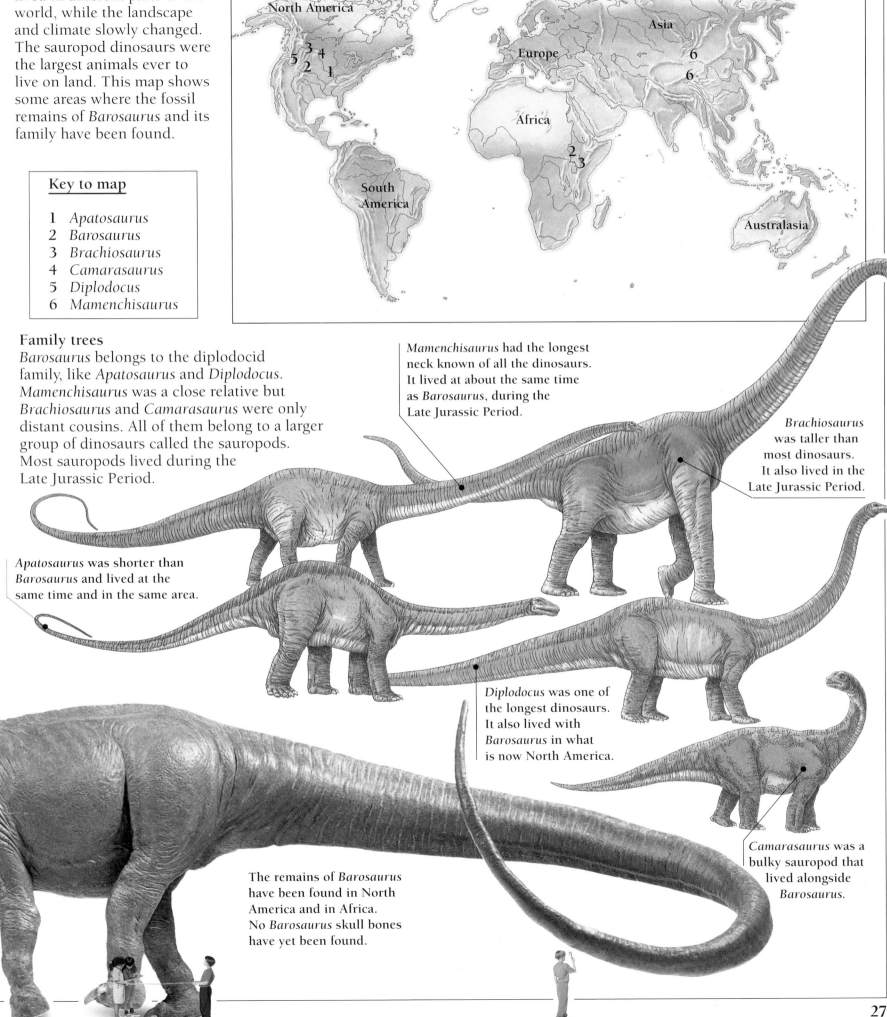

Key to map

1 *Apatosaurus*
2 *Barosaurus*
3 *Brachiosaurus*
4 *Camarasaurus*
5 *Diplodocus*
6 *Mamenchisaurus*

North America

Asia

Europe

Africa

South America

Australasia

Family trees

Barosaurus belongs to the diplodocid family, like *Apatosaurus* and *Diplodocus*. *Mamenchisaurus* was a close relative but *Brachiosaurus* and *Camarasaurus* were only distant cousins. All of them belong to a larger group of dinosaurs called the sauropods. Most sauropods lived during the Late Jurassic Period.

Mamenchisaurus had the longest neck known of all the dinosaurs. It lived at about the same time as *Barosaurus*, during the Late Jurassic Period.

Brachiosaurus was taller than most dinosaurs. It also lived in the Late Jurassic Period.

Apatosaurus was shorter than *Barosaurus* and lived at the same time and in the same area.

Diplodocus was one of the longest dinosaurs. It also lived with *Barosaurus* in what is now North America.

Camarasaurus was a bulky sauropod that lived alongside *Barosaurus*.

The remains of *Barosaurus* have been found in North America and in Africa. No *Barosaurus* skull bones have yet been found.

27

GLOSSARY

carnivore
A meat-eating animal.

cast
A replica of a fossil, made from a mold.

Cretaceous Period
Part of the Earth's history, which lasted from 145 million years ago until 65 million years ago, when the dinosaurs became extinct.

dinosaurs
A group of extinct, land-living reptiles that lived on Earth from 230 until 65 million years ago.

duck-billed dinosaur
Another name for a hadrosaur, a dinosaur with a ducklike beak.

environment
The land, water, climate, animals, and plants that surround a living thing, and affect how it lives.

excavate
To dig up an object such as a fossil.

extinction
When living things, such as dinosaurs, die and disappear from the Earth forever.

formation
A group of rock layers recognizable as a unit.

fossil
Part of a dead plant or animal that has been buried and has been turned as hard as stone by chemicals in the rock around it.

gastrolith
A stone swallowed by a dinosaur and used in part of its stomach to help grind up tough plants.

fiberglass
Compressed fibrous glass used to strengthen the plastic used in making fossil casts.

herbivore
A plant-eating animal.

impression
A copy of the shape of a fossil and the marks on its surface.

Jurassic Period
Part of the Earth's history from 208 to 145 million years ago. *Barosaurus* lived during this Period.

mold
The impression from which a cast of a fossil is made.

ornithischian dinosaur
The bird-hipped type of dinosaur with both lower hip bones pointing down and backward.

paleontologist
A scientist who studies fossils and life in ancient times.

pelvis
The group of bones where the legs join the backbone of an animal's skeleton.

replica
A copy of something.

reptile
A scaly animal that lays eggs, such as the turtles, snakes, lizards, and crocodiles of today. The dinosaurs were reptiles.

saurischian dinosaur
The lizard-hipped type of dinosaur with one of the two lower hip bones pointing down and forward; the other bone points backward and down.

sauropod
A group of large, plant-eating, lizard-hipped dinosaurs, such as *Barosaurus*.

scavenger
A meat-eater that feeds on prey that is already dead, rather than on prey that it has killed.

skeleton
The supporting bony frame inside an animal's body.

specimen
An example of one kind of plant or animal, or a part of it.

Triassic Period
Part of the Earth's history, which lasted from 245 to 208 million years ago. Dinosaurs first appeared in this Period.

vertebrae
Bones that form the backbone of animals.

weathering
When rocks and soil are broken up and washed or blown away by wind, rain, sun, frost, and other features of the weather.

Pronunciation guide to the dinosaur names in this book

- *Allosaurus* (al-low-saw-rus)
- *Apatosaurus* (ah-pat-oh-saw-rus)
- *Barosaurus* (barrow-saw-rus)
- *Brachiosaurus* (brakky-oh-saw-rus)
- *Camarasaurus* (kam-ah-ra-saw-rus)
- *Camptosaurus* (camp-toe-saw-rus)
- *Cetiosaurus* (seaty-oh-saw-rus)
- *Diplodocus* (di-plod-ock-us)
- *Dryosaurus* (dry-oh-saw-rus)
- *Heterodontosaurus* (het-ter-row-dont-oh-saw-rus)
- *Mamenchisaurus* (mammenky-saw-rus)
- *Stegosaurus* (stegg-oh-saw-rus)
- *Struthiomimus* (strewth-ee-yo-meem-us)

INDEX

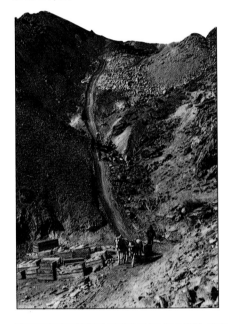

ACKNOWLEDGMENTS

Picture credits
t=top b=bottom m=middle l=left r=right
Courtesy Department of Library Services, American Museum of Natural History: Neg. no. 37243, 13mr; The Carnegie Museum of Natural History: Neg. no. 1012, 11br; Special Collections, University of Utah Library: Neg. no. 860, 10bml; Neg. no. 815, 12tl; Neg. no. 763, 12m (upper); Neg. no. 798, 12m (lower); Neg. no. 815, 12bm; Neg. no. 1039, 12br; Neg. no. 860, 28br; Neg. no. 1039, 29ml.
Model photography by Dave King 4, 5, 6bl, 6br, 7, 20bl, 22–25, 29br. Museum photography by Lynton Gardiner 8bl, 8tr, 8mr, 11tl, 12bl, 12tr, 12mr, 13bl, 14–21, 26mr, 28tr, 28bl, 29tr, 29mr.

Additional special photography by Paul Bricknell (magnifying glass) 11br, 29mr; Andy Crawford (children) 5, 20, 21, 27; Colin Keates 24mr; Mary Ann Lynch 16tr; Tim Ridley 6tl, 6tr, 14t, 14mr, 15tl, 26b, 27b; Jerry Young 9mr.
Barosaurus scale model, 20tr, courtesy of Eugene Gaffney; designed by Shinobu Matsumura; manufactured by Kaiyodo Company Ltd, Japan.
Index by Lynn Bresler.
Dorling Kindersley would like to thank Mandy Earey, Jonathan Buckley, Sharon Peters, Scarlett Lovell, Eugene Gaffney,

Elizabeth Chapman, Mick Ellison, Andrea La Sala, Tony Pollo, and Peter May and the folks at Research Casting for their help in producing this book. Thanks also to Roger Priddy for art directing photography at the American Museum of Natural History.
Thanks also to Jennie Joannides, Natalie Ebrey, Jamie Ross, Darren Chin, and Daniel Ray for appearing in this book.

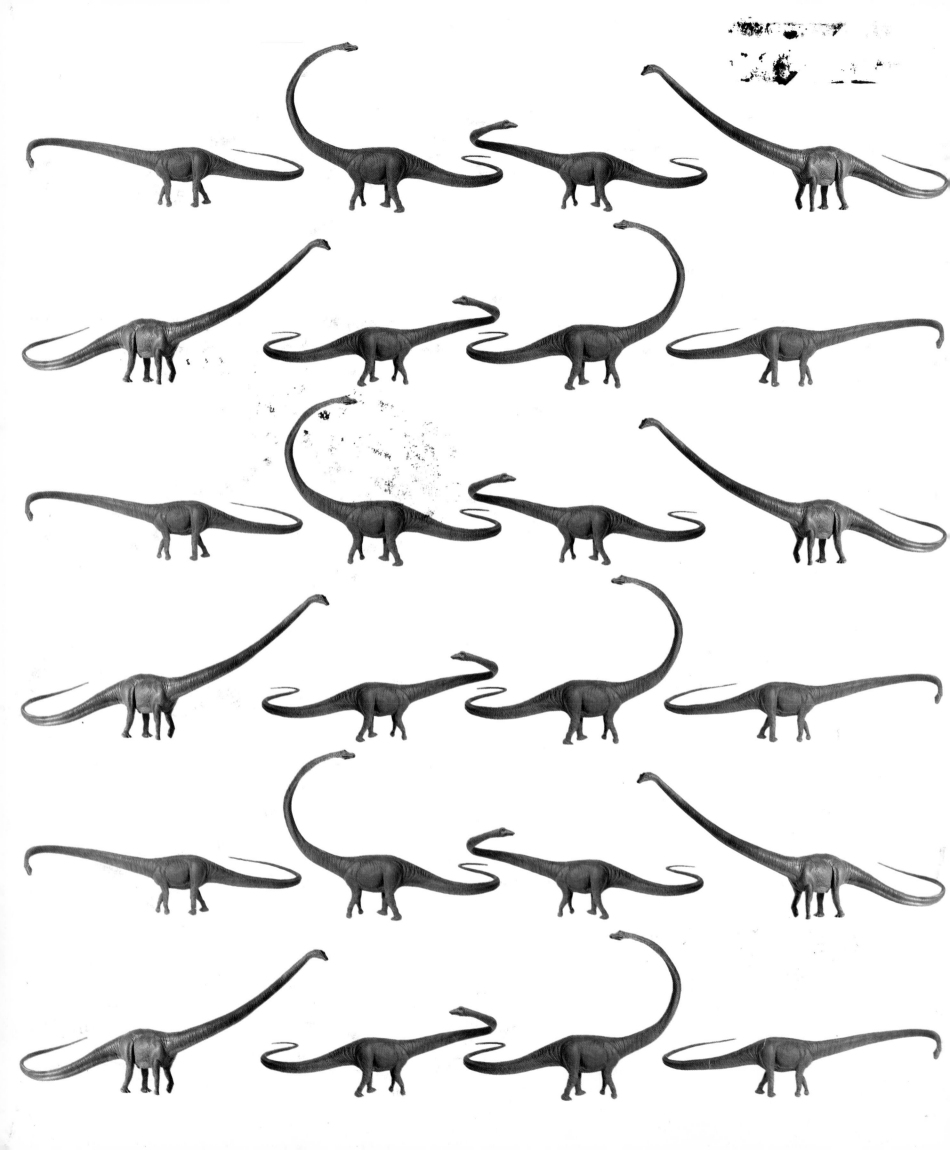